interactive
SCIENCE

A kitten's eyes often change color as the kitten grows.

PEARSON

Glenview, Illinois • Boston, Massachusetts • Chandler, Arizona • New York, New York

ISBN-13: 978-0-328-87136-0
ISBN-10: 0-328-87136-2
9   18

Program Authors

DON BUCKLEY, M.Sc.
Director of Technology & Innovation,
The School at Columbia University,
New York, New York
Don Buckley has transformed learning spaces, textbooks, and media resources so that they work for students and teachers. He has advanced degrees from leading European universities, is a former industrial chemist, published photographer, and former consultant to MOMA's Education Department. He also teaches a graduate course at Columbia Teacher's College in Educational Technology and directs the Technology and Innovation program at the school. He is passionate about travel, architecture, design, change, the future, and innovation.

ZIPPORAH MILLER, M.A.Ed.
Coordinator for K-12 Science Programs,
Anne Arundel County Public Schools.
Mrs. Zipporah Miller served as a reviewer during the development of the Next Generation Science Standards and provides national training to teachers, administrators, higher education staff, and informal science stakeholders on the Next Generation Science Standards. Prior to her appointment in Anne Arundel, Mrs. Miller served as the Associate Executive Director for Professional Development Programs and Conferences at the National Science Teachers Association (NSTA).

MICHAEL J. PADILLA, Ph.D.
Eugene P. Moore School of Education,
Clemson University, Clemson,
South Carolina
A former middle school teacher and a leader in middle school science education, Dr. Michael Padilla has served as president of the National Science Teachers Association and reviewed the Next Generation Science Standards. He is a former professor of science education at Clemson University. As lead author of the *Science Explorer* series, Dr. Padilla has inspired the team in developing a program that promotes student inquiry and meets the needs of today's students.

KATHRYN THORNTON, Ph.D.
Professor, Mechanical & Aerospace
Engineering, University of Virginia,
Charlottesville, Virginia
Selected by NASA in May 1984, Dr. Kathryn Thornton is a veteran of four space flights. She has logged more than 975 hours in space, including more than 21 hours of extravehicular activity. As an author on the *Scott Foresman Science* series, Dr. Thornton's enthusiasm for science has inspired teachers around the globe.

MICHAEL E. WYSESSION, Ph.D.
Associate Professor of Earth and
Planetary Science, Washington University,
St. Louis, Missouri
An author on more than 50 scientific publications, Dr. Wysession was awarded the prestigious Packard Foundation Fellowship and Presidential Faculty Fellowship for his research in geophysics. Dr. Wysession is an expert on Earth's inner structure and has mapped various regions of Earth using seismic tomography. He is known internationally for his work in geoscience education and research, and was a lead writer of the Earth and Space Science Next Generation Science Standards.

Instructional Design Author
GRANT WIGGINS, Ed.D.
President, Authentic Education,
Hopewell, New Jersey

Activities Author
KAREN L. OSTLUND, Ph.D.
Past President, National Science
Teachers Association, Arlington, Virginia

ELL Consultant
JIM CUMMINGS, Ph.D.
Professor and Canada Research Chair,
Curriculum, Teaching and Learning
department at the University of Toronto

Chapter 1

Motion

Chapter 2

Living Things

? What do plants and animals need?

Chapter 3

Earth and Sky

The Nature of Science

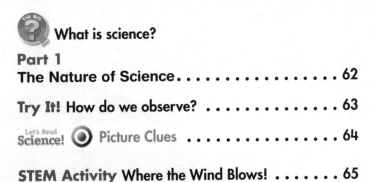

? **What is science?**

Solve Problems

Chapter
1

Motion

How does the ball move?

Name _____

What are position and motion?

Look at each picture.

Circle the person who made the ball move.

 **Draw** an arrow where you think the ball will go.

Directions: Discuss how each picture shows a ball in motion. Then have children circle the person who made the ball move in the first picture. Guide them in using the motion lines to help predict where the ball will go. Have them draw an arrow to show their prediction. Repeat the procedure for the second picture.

 Home Activity: Demonstrate different types of motion using a ball. Toss, kick, and roll a ball back and forth with your child.

How do objects move?

You need

journal

rolling toy

paper

pencil

1 Move.

2 Trace.

3 Observe.

4  Draw.

Name _____

How do objects move?

 Draw how objects move.

 Directions: Have children roll a ball or push a toy across a solid surface and draw what happens when the ball rolls away from them.

⊙ Cause and Effect
What made the swing move?

Let's Read Science!

Cause and Effect

Look at what happened in each row.

(Circle) the picture that shows why it happened.

 **Activity 3**
Use with page 3.

 Directions: Tell children that the first picture in each row shows what has happened. Have children tell what they see in the first picture in row 1. Then have children circle the picture that shows why the balloon is in the air. Continue in the same way for rows 2 and 3.

 Home Activity: Demonstrate examples of cause-and-effect relationships in the home. For example, dirty dishes get clean because they are washed, and a light turns off because you flick a switch.

Move Around It!

You want to roll a ball across the floor to a partner.

Other things are in the way.

How can you roll the ball around them?

Find a Problem

1  **Circle** the problem.

Plan and Draw

2 Where does the ball need to go?

Draw a path.

Choose Materials

3 You will build something to make the ball follow the path.

 Circle the materials you will use.

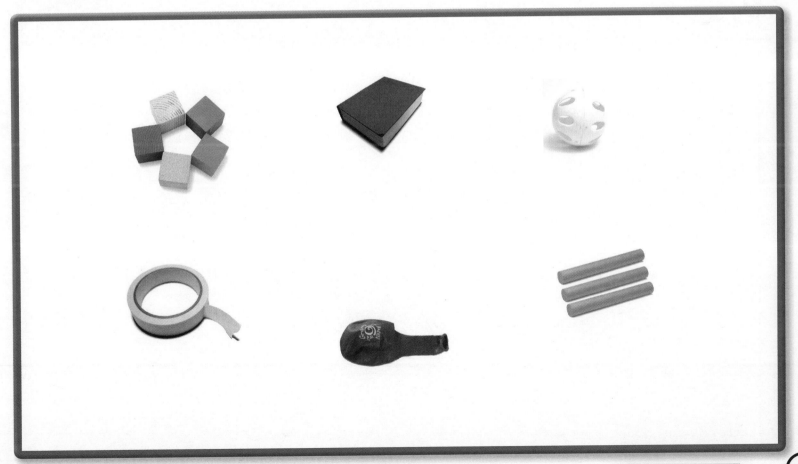

4 **Draw** one material you will not use.

Tell why.

Make and Test

5 **Draw** how you will use your materials.

6 Build something that will make the ball follow the path.

7 Push your ball to follow the path.

What happens?

Draw.

Record and Share

8 Tell about your path.

Did the path help the ball change direction?

9 Give your ball a soft push.

Did the ball reach your partner?

 **Circle**

Yes	No

10 Give your ball a hard push.

Did the ball reach your partner?

 | Yes | No |

11 How hard do you need to push the ball to make it reach your partner?

 | Soft push | Hard push |

12 Look at someone else's path. **Compare.**

Whose ball reached a partner?

Circle

My ball	Another child's ball
Both balls	Neither ball

13 **Draw** how someone else's path is different.

14 **Plan** your path again.

Draw how it is different.

Lesson 1

What can you tell about an object's position?

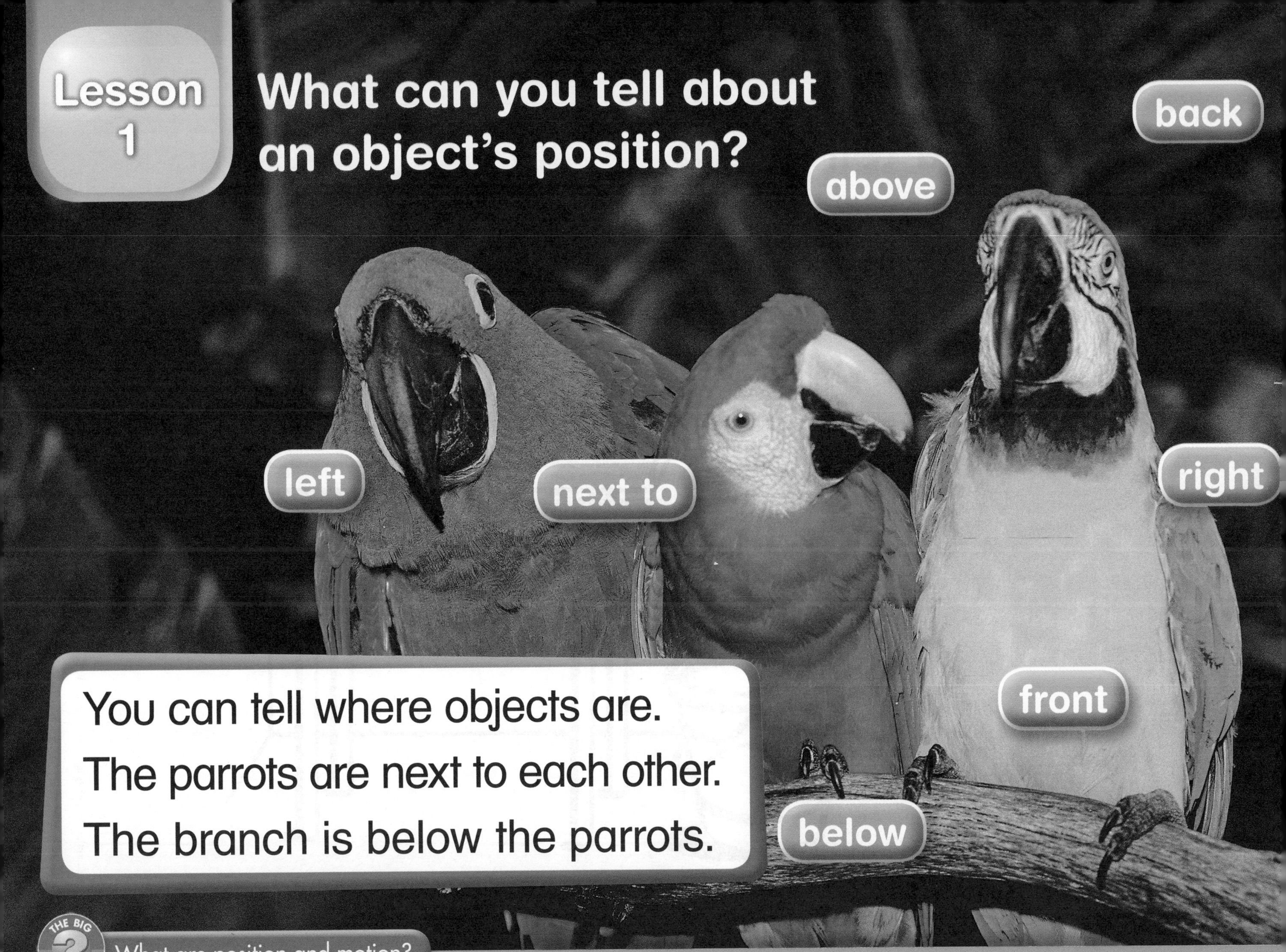
back
above
left
next to
right
front
below

You can tell where objects are.
The parrots are next to each other.
The branch is below the parrots.

THE BIG ? What are position and motion?

Name _____

What can you tell about an object's position?

 Draw an ✗ on the object next to the table.

 Color the object below the pitcher.

 **Directions:** Discuss with children the position of the objects in the picture. Guide them in understanding the relationships between *above/below, front/back,* and *right/left.* Then have children identify the table, pitcher, spool of thread, and the bucket.

Home Activity: Use household objects to help your child practice identifying position. Point to an object and ask your child to describe its position relative to another object. For example, point to an overhead light and ask if the light is above or below the table.

What makes objects move?

You can use a push to move an object.
You can use a pull to move an object.
A push or a pull can change how
an object moves.

THE BIG ? What are position and motion?

Name _____

What makes objects move?

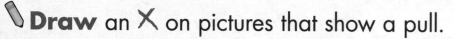 pictures that show a push.

 Draw an ✗ on pictures that show a pull.

 Directions: Have children identify each picture and tell whether it shows a push or a pull. Then have children circle pictures showing pushes and put an X on pictures showing pulls.

 Home Activity: Have your child use a toy to demonstrate pushes and pulls.

What are some ways objects move?

Objects may move fast or slowly.
A big push or pull can speed up an object.
A big push or pull can slow down an object.
Look at these objects.
Put the objects in order from slowest to fastest.

THE BIG ? What are position and motion?

What are some ways objects move?

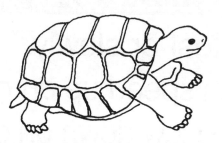

✏️ **Color** things that move fast blue.

✏️ **Color** things that move slowly red.

Activity 16
Use with page 16.

Directions: Discuss *fast* and *slow* as opposites. Then have children identify and color the animals, objects, and people that move fast blue and those that move slowly red. Talk about what makes objects move faster or slower.

Home Activity: Play an outdoors speed game with your child. Name something that moves fast, such as a train, and have your child run. Continue by naming fast- and slow-moving things and having your child run or walk to show how each thing moves.

How do moving objects affect each other?

Moving objects can run into each other.

Then they push on each other.

The push changes how the objects move.

The objects might start moving or stop moving.

They might speed up or slow down.

They might change direction.

THE BIG ? What are position and motion?

Name _____

How do moving objects affect each other?

The two balls roll into each other.

 Draw arrows to show what will happen to the two balls.

Color the picture.

 **Directions:** Have children identify which way the balls will move in the picture. Then have children draw arrows to show what will happen to the balls.

 Home Activity: Have your child use balls, toys, or other objects to demonstrate how moving objects affect each other.

How can you move the car?

You need

journal

car

1 Push.
Push hard.
Tell.

2 Pull.
Pull hard.
Tell.

3 Draw.

Name _____

How can you move the car?

 **Draw.**

Circle push or pull.

push pull	push pull

Activity 18
Use with page 18.

 Directions: Have children draw a hand pushing the car and then circle *push*. Have children draw a hand pulling the car and then circle *pull*.

Slide Engineer

Slides can be made by engineers.

The engineer uses math.

The engineer uses technology.

The engineer makes the slide fun.

The engineer makes the slide safe.

THE BIG
? What are position and motion?

Name _____

Slide Engineer

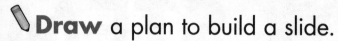 **Draw** a plan to build a slide.

STEM

 Directions: Review with children how engineers make slides. Tell children that engineers make a plan first. Have children draw a plan for a slide and share their pictures.

 Home Activity: Talk with your child about things you plan around the house, such as what to make for dinner. Plan a household task with your child. Have your child assist in writing or drawing your plan.

Chapter 2

Living Things

Where do these animals get food?

THE BIG ? What do plants and animals need?

Name _____

Living Things

Circle pictures of living things.

 Directions: Identify each picture in the box. Then have children circle the pictures of living things.

 Home Activity: As you walk with your child, take turns identifying living things.

Do plants need water?

You need

plant

water

1 Observe.

2 Predict.

3 Wait.

4 Draw.

Name _____

Do plants need water?

Draw the plant before and after it is watered.

Before Water	After Water

Activity 21
Use with page 21.

Directions: Ask children to predict what might happen after they add water to the plant. In the first column, have children draw a picture of the plant before they add water. In the second column, tell children to draw a picture of the plant after they add water. Discuss what would happen if the plant did not get water.

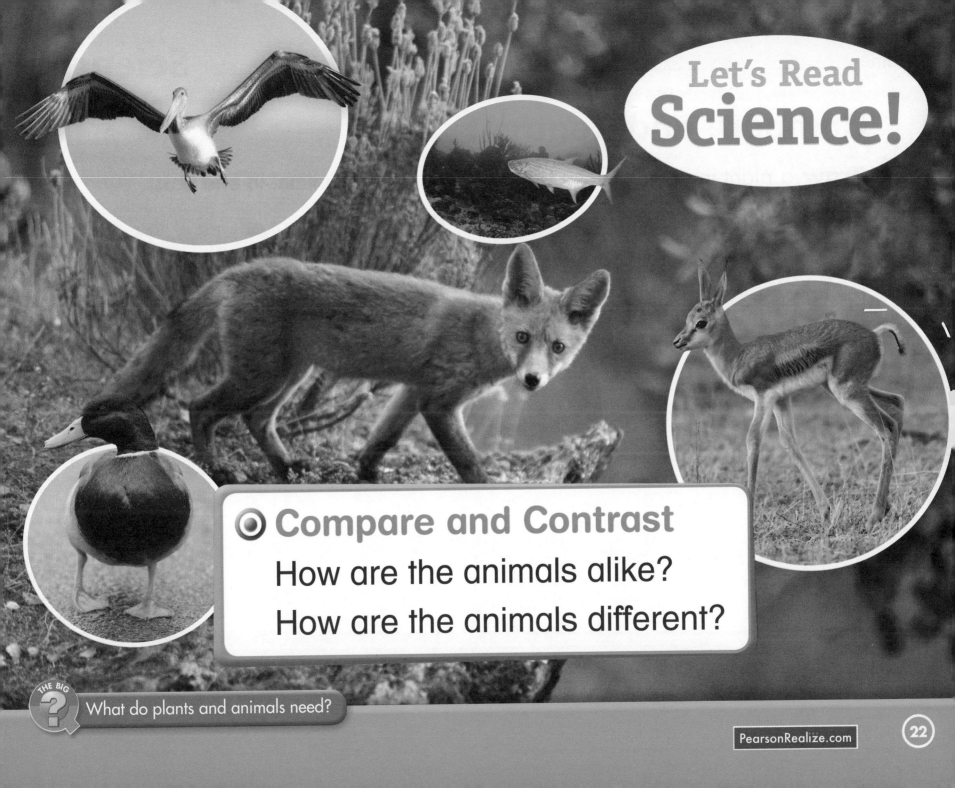

Let's Read
Science!

◉ **Compare and Contrast**

How are the animals alike?

How are the animals different?

Name _____

Compare and Contrast

 **Draw** a plant in one box.

Draw a different plant in the other box.

Tell how the two plants are alike.

 **Draw** an animal in one box.

Draw a different animal in the other box.

Tell how the two animals are alike.

 Directions: Have children think of two plants they can draw. Offer suggestions or show pictures, if necessary. When children have finished drawing, have them tell how their two plants are alike and different. Repeat with two animals.

Home Activity: Show your child pictures of two different kinds of plants. Take turns telling how the plants are alike and different.

Scratch Away!

Cats have claws.

Cats need to trim their claws.

Cats can trim their claws on a scratch post.

Find a Problem

1 Circle the claws on the cat.

2 What can the cat use to trim its claws?

Draw.

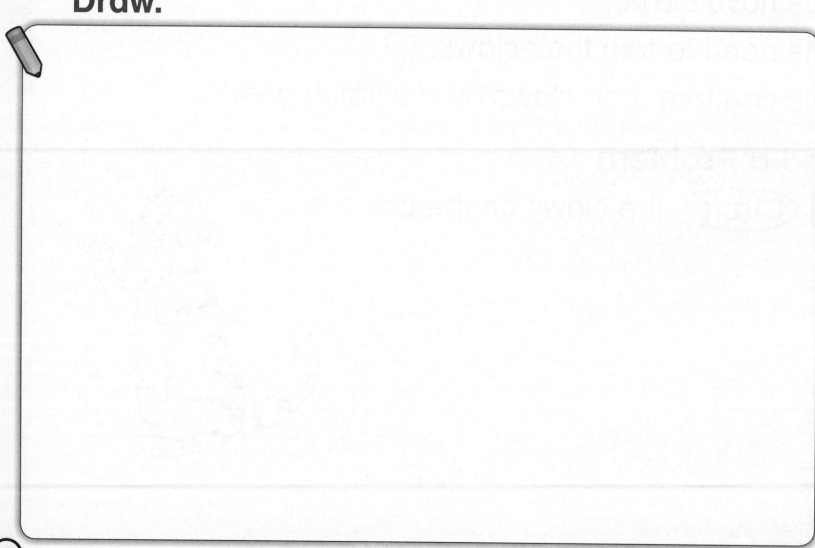

Plan and Draw

3 What does a long cat claw look like?

Draw.

4 What will your scratching post look like?

Draw.

Choose Materials

5 Write yes or no.

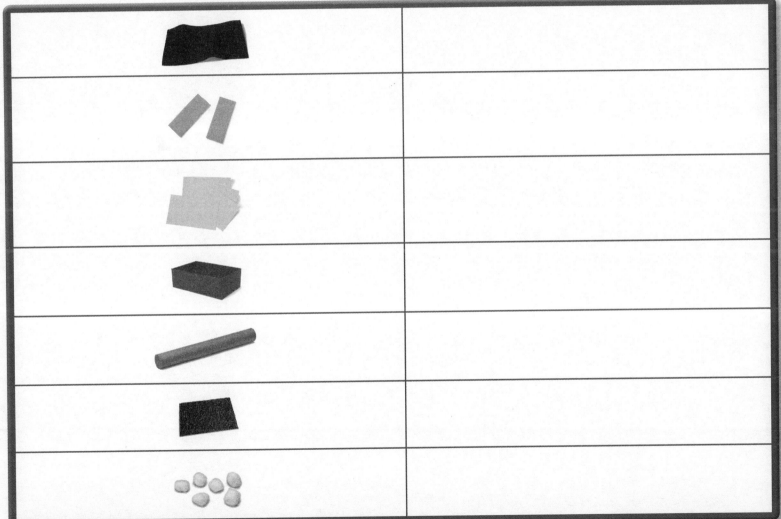

6 **Draw** one material you did not use. Tell why.

Make and Test

7 **Draw** how you will use your materials.

8 Build your scratching post.

9 How can you test your scratching post?

Circle an example.

Record and Share

10 Tell about your scratching post.

Did it work?

11 Look at another scratching post.

Draw or tell how it is different.

12 **Plan** your scratching post again.

How is it different?

Draw.

What are nonliving things?

Nonliving things do not grow.

Nonliving things do not change or move on their own.

Look around.

You will see many nonliving things.

 What do plants and animals need?

Name _____

What are nonliving things?

(**Circle**) the nonliving thing in each row.

 Directions: Help children identify the pictures in each row. Then have them circle the picture that shows a nonliving thing.

Home Activity: Point out living and nonliving things in your environment, such as a tree and a stop sign. Ask your child which is the nonliving thing.

What are living things?

Living things grow.

Living things change or move on their own.

Plants and animals are living things.

You are a living thing too.

Look around.

You will see many living things.

Name _____

What are living things?

Circle the two living things in the picture.

Color the picture.

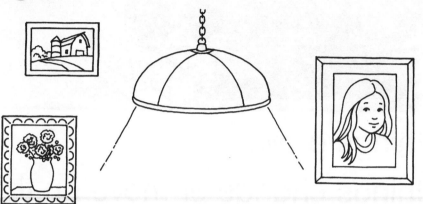

 Directions: Discuss with children how living things differ from nonliving things. Then ask children to circle the two living things in the picture. Encourage children to color the picture.

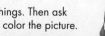 **Home Activity:** Help your child identify living things in and around your home.

What do plants need?

Plants need air.

Plants need water.

Plants need light to make food.

Plants need space to live and grow.

THE BIG ? What do plants and animals need?

Name _____

What do plants need?

 Draw what you think the grown plant will look like.

 Color your picture.

water

and

soil

and

light

 Directions: Discuss what plants need. Encourage children to draw a full-grown plant with stems and leaves in the pot. Help them understand that soil, water, and light help plants grow healthy.

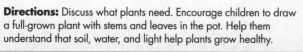 **Home Activity:** Help your child notice plants in your neighborhood that are getting what they need.

What do animals need?

Animals need air and water.

Animals need food.

Animals use plants and other animals as food.

They get nutrients from food.

Animals live in places where they can get what they need.

THE BIG ? What do plants and animals need?

Name _____

What do animals need?

 Draw the things the animal needs.

Directions: Discuss the things that animals need. Have children draw the dog's needs in the picture. Remind them that air is also a need, though they may not be able to draw this.

Home Activity: Show your child pictures of plants and animals and discuss how their needs are the same and different.

What do you need?

People need air and water.

People need food.

People get nutrients from food.

People find what they need in the world around them.

THE BIG ?

What do plants and animals need?

Lesson 5

Name _____

What do you need?

Color the picture of the boy meeting a need.

Directions: Ask children to color the picture that shows the boy doing something he needs to do to live.

Home Activity: Let your child help you feed a pet or pour a glass of juice. Talk about how living things need food, water, air, and space to live.

How do living things affect where they live?

Living things make changes to meet their needs.

Tree roots can break rocks as the roots grow.

Groundhogs dig tunnels in the ground for shelter.

Woodpeckers poke holes in trees to find food.

People clear land to build homes.

THE BIG ? What do plants and animals need?

How do living things affect where they live?

Look at each picture.

 Draw how an animal would change the land and water to meet a need.

 Directions: Ask children to look at the pictures of land and water and draw how an animal would change each environment to meet a need.

 Home Activity: Go outside with your child and look around. Discuss plants and animals you see. Talk about how these plants and animals make changes where they live in order to meet needs.

How do some turtles stay warm in winter?

You need

plastic cup with thermometer

plastic cup with thermometer and soil

cooler (whole class use)

red crayon

Thermometer Chart

1 Record.

2 Put.

3 Predict.

4 Wait.

5 Record.

Name _____

How do some turtles stay warm in winter?

Draw a picture showing where turtles might live in the winter.

Activity 39
Use with page 39.

Directions: Help children understand that some turtles might live in the soil during the winter because it stays warmer.

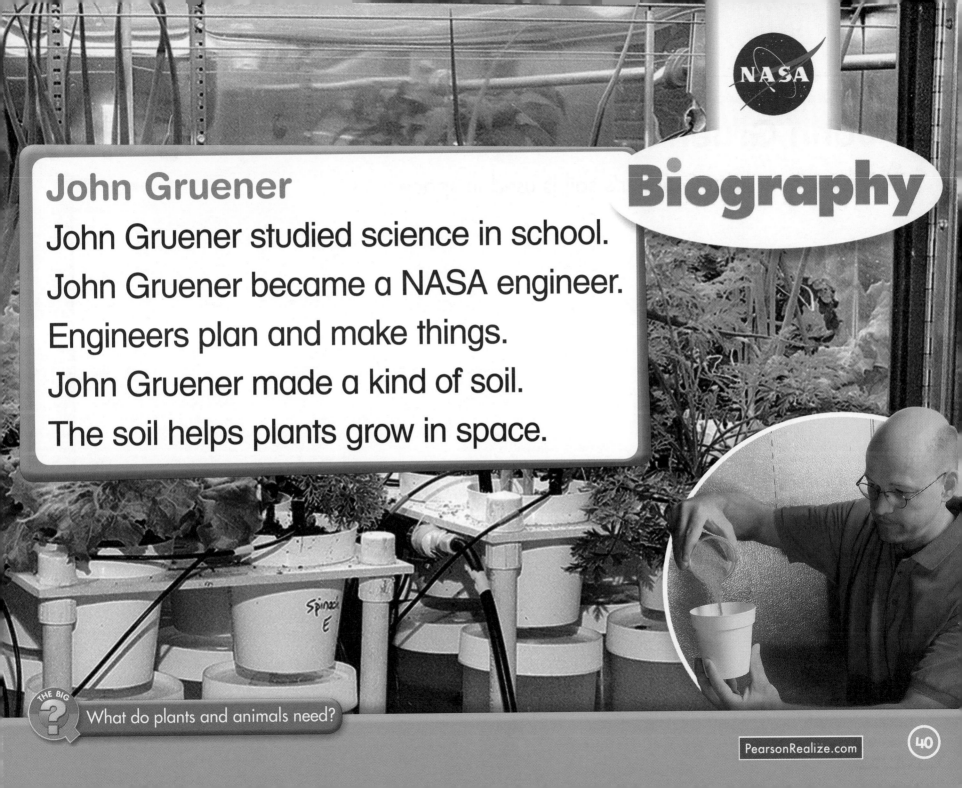

John Gruener

John Gruener studied science in school.

John Gruener became a NASA engineer.

Engineers plan and make things.

John Gruener made a kind of soil.

The soil helps plants grow in space.

THE BIG
? What do plants and animals need?

John Gruener

Biography

 Draw how John Gruener's soil is used in space.

 Directions: Review with children how John Gruener's soil is used in space. Have children share their pictures.

 Home Activity: Your child has learned about what living things need and how they meet these needs. Help your child plant and care for a seed. Watch as it grows. Talk with your child about how the plant gets what it needs.

Earth and Sky

Is it

night

or

day?

THE BIG
?

What are Earth and the sky like?

Name _____

What are Earth and sky like?

Look at the pictures.

Color the picture that shows what the chapter is about.

 Directions: Then have children color the picture on this page that shows what this chapter is about.

 Home Activity: In this chapter, your child will learn about the sky and the objects that can be seen in the sky. Take time to look at the daytime sky with your child. Talk about what you see. Do you see clouds, the sun, airplanes, or birds?

How does weather change?

You need

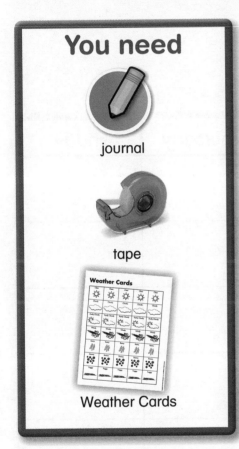

journal

tape

Weather Cards

1 Observe the weather.

2  Record.

3 Count.

	Monday	Tuesday	Wednesday	Thursday	Friday
Clear					
Cloudy					
Partly cloudy					
Windy					
Rainy or snowy					
Foggy					

Name _____

How does weather change?

✏ **Record.**

	Monday	Tuesday	Wednesday	Thursday	Friday
Clear ☀					
Cloudy ☁					
Partly Cloudy 🌤					
Rainy or snowy 🌧❄					
Windy 🌬					
Foggy 🌫					

Activity 42
Use with page 42.

 Directions: Have children check the box for the type of weather they see each day. Have them record the weather each week for one month.

◉ **Draw Conclusions**

What was the weather like here?

How do you know?

Draw Conclusions

Look at the picture of a place on Earth.

(Circle) the picture that tells what the weather is usually like in this place.

Activity 43
Use with page 43.

Directions: Discuss the place shown in the large picture. Then ask children to use what they know and the picture to draw conclusions about the weather in this place. Have children circle the small picture that shows what the weather is like.

Home Activity: Help your child practice drawing conclusions using weather-specific clothing, such as raincoats, mittens, shorts, umbrellas, and sweaters. Display the clothing and ask your child when he or she would wear it and why.

Cool Down!

The sky is bright.

The sand in the sandbox is hot.

You wish you felt cooler.

Find a Problem

1 The heat comes from something in the sky.

(Circle) where the heat comes from.

2 You would be cooler if you could block the heat.

Where would you put something to block the heat?

Circle

Above sandbox	Next to sandbox	Under sandbox

Plan and Draw

3 How could you make the sandbox cooler?

Draw.

4 You can build a model of a sandbox.

How can you protect your model from the hot sun?

Draw.

Choose Materials

5 Write yes next to the materials you will use.

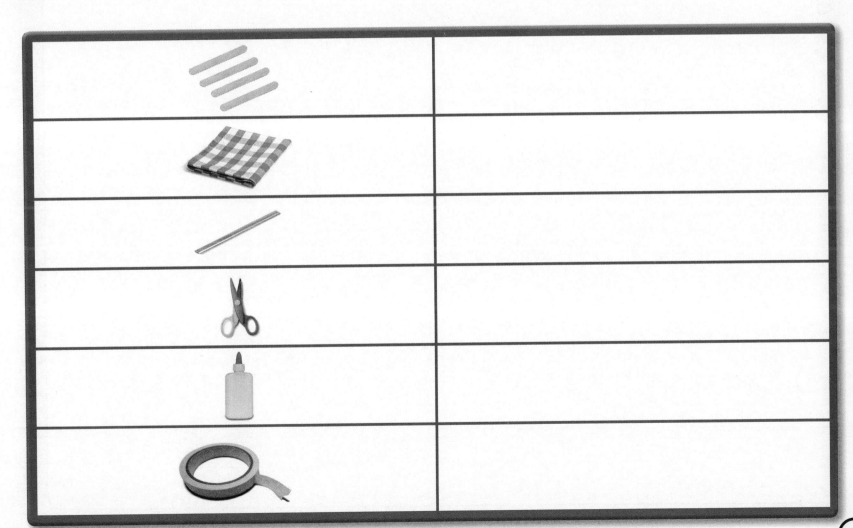

6 **Draw** one material you did not use. Tell why.

Make and Test

7 **Draw** how you will use your materials.

8 Put sand in a bowl. This is a model of a sandbox.

9 Build a sun blocker to protect your model from the sun's heat.

10 Let the sun shine on your model sandbox without the sun blocker.

Wait 5 minutes.

Feel the sand.
How does it feel?

Cool	Warm

11 Put the sun blocker on your model sandbox.

Let the sun shine on your model sandbox for 5 minutes.

12 Feel the sand.
How does it feel?

Cool	Warm

Record and Share

13 Tell about your sun blocker.

Did it work?

Yes	No

14 Look at a partner's sun blocker. **Compare.**

Draw or tell how it is different.

15 **Plan** another sun blocker.

Draw how it is different.

What can you see in the day sky?

You can see clouds and the sun in the day sky.
Sometimes you can see the moon in the day sky.
Tell about objects in the day sky.

THE BIG ? What are Earth and the sky like?

Name _____

What can you see in the day sky?

(Circle) the objects you might see in the day sky.

Activity 54
Use with page 54.

Directions: Have children identify each picture. Then have children circle the objects they can see in the sky during the day. Review the page, emphasizing that sometimes the moon can be seen in the day sky and sometimes it can be seen in the night sky. Ask which object is never seen in the sky.

Home Activity: Your child identified things that can be seen in the daytime sky. Together with your child, discuss what you would see in the daytime sky. Then draw a picture of the objects in the sky.

How does the sun seem to move?

The sun looks low in the morning sky.

The sun looks high in the sky at noon.

The sun looks low in the evening sky.

noon

evening

morning

THE BIG
?
What are Earth and the sky like?

Name _____

How does the sun seem to move?

✏️ **Draw** the sun. Show the sun in the early morning sky.

✏️ **Draw** the sun. Show the sun in the sky at noon.

✏️ **Draw** the sun. Show the sun in the early evening sky.

Activity 55
Use with page 55.

 Directions: Read the directions for the first picture to children. Help them identify where to draw the sun. Then have them draw the sun. Repeat the process for the second and third pictures.

 Home Activity: Together with your child look at the sky at different times of day. Draw pictures showing where the sun is at each time. Write the time on each picture.

What do you get from the sun?

The sun shines on Earth.

You get light from the sun.

We use light from the sun to see.

Plants use light from the sun to grow.

The sun makes you warm.

The sun warms the land.

The sun warms the water.

The sun warms the air.

Living things need heat from the sun.

What are Earth and the sky like?

Name _____

What do you get from the sun?

✏️ **Draw** something you do outdoors on a warm, sunny day.

Activity 56
Use with page 56.

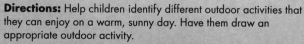 **Directions:** Help children identify different outdoor activities that they can enjoy on a warm, sunny day. Have them draw an appropriate outdoor activity.

 Home Activity: Write the words *Sun Fun* at the top of a sheet of paper. Have your child draw a picture showing something he or she can do to have fun outdoors on a sunny day.

The weather can change every day.

The weather may be sunny, cloudy, windy, rainy, or snowy.

You can show the weather on a calendar.

Show what the weather is like today.

April

Sunday	Monday	Tuesday	Wednesday	Thursday	Friday	Saturday
			1	2	3	
4	5	6	7	8	9	10
11	12	13	14	15	16	17
18	19	20	21	22	23	24
25	26	27	28	29	30	

THE BIG **?** What are Earth and the sky like?

Name _____

What are some kinds of weather?

Color the picture that best shows
what the weather is like today.

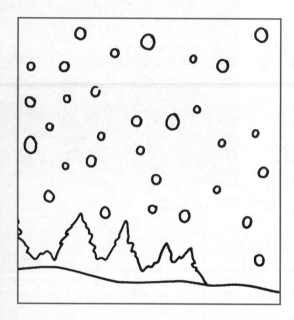

Directions: Look at the pictures with children. Discuss the type of
weather each picture shows and the weather children observed today.
Then have them color the picture that best matches today's weather.

Home Activity: Discuss these kinds of weather with your child:
sunny, cloudy, windy, rainy, and snowy. Have your child draw a
picture of himself or herself outdoors in today's weather.

How can we use rocks, soil, and water?

We use rocks to build.

We build houses, walls, and roads.

We use soil to grow plants for food.

We use water to drink, wash, cook, and clean.

THE BIG
What are Earth and the sky like?

Name _____

How can we use rocks, soil, and water?

 **Draw** a line to match each word with the correct picture.

 rocks   soil   water

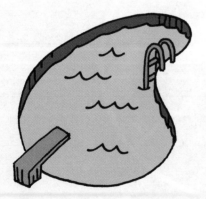

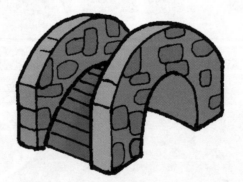

 **Directions:** Review with children the uses of rocks, soil, and water in the lesson text. Discuss how these Earth materials are being used in the pictures on this page. Have children draw lines to match the words with the appropriate pictures.

 Home Activity: Talk with your child about ways rocks, soil, and water are useful at home. Together, make three lists, one for each Earth material.

When we recycle, we do not throw things away. Recycling helps care for Earth. We reuse old things to make new things.

You can recycle.

Save paper, plastic, and metal. They can be made into new things.

What can you recycle?

Circle the objects you can recycle. Put an X on the objects you can't recycle.

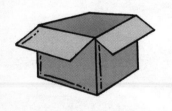

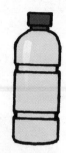

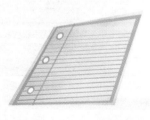

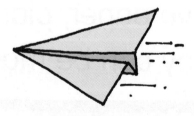

Activity 59
Use with page 59.

Directions: Review with children what kinds of objects can be recycled and what items can't be recycled. Explain that we recycle to conserve natural resources and materials. Then have children circle the objects on the page that can be recycled. Have children draw an X on objects that can't be recycled.

Home Activity: With your child, gather objects made of paper, plastic, and metal. Take turns demonstrating how to use, conserve, and dispose of the materials by reusing or recycling the objects.

How can the sun make temperatures change?

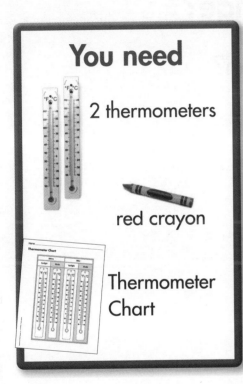

You need

2 thermometers

red crayon

Thermometer Chart

1 Look.

2 Color.

3 Put.

4 Wait.
Look.

5 Color.

Name _____

How can the sun make temperatures change?

Circle Did sunlight make the temperature go up or down?

Up

Down

Activity 60
Use with page 60.

 Directions: Have children complete the thermometer activity. Then discuss which thermometer warmed up more. Guide children to look at their thermometer charts and circle the correct answer on the page.

Big World My World

Big World

Ready for the Weather

People learn about the weather across the country.

You learn about the weather too.

Some places have more severe weather than others.

Weather scientists tell people when severe weather is expected so they can prepare.

What do you do to get ready for stormy weather?

My World

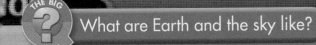

What are Earth and the sky like?

Name _____

Ready for the Weather

 **Color** the picture that shows what you could wear and use on a hot summer day.

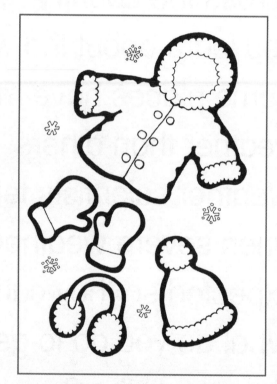

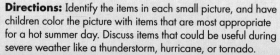 **Directions:** Identify the items in each small picture, and have children color the picture with items that are most appropriate for a hot summer day. Discuss items that could be useful during severe weather like a thunderstorm, hurricane, or tornado.

 Home Activity: Discuss with your child types of severe weather—thunderstorms, blizzards, tornadoes, and hurricanes, for example—that can happen where you live. Describe what he or she should do if weather scientists say that weather is on its way.

The Nature of Science

Why is she looking so closely?

THE BIG ? What is science?

Name _____

What is science?

 Draw a picture in the hand lens.

Directions: Discuss observation as a practice of science, and talk about what the girl might see through the hand lens. Then have children draw a picture of a flower in the hand lens on this page.

Home Activity: Your child is studying the practices of science. One practice is to observe things and tell about them. Hold up an object, and ask your child to tell something about it. Then reverse roles with your child.

How do we observe?

You need

journal

hand lens

objects

1 Look.

2 Tell 3 things.

3 Repeat.

4 Draw.

Name _____

How do we observe?

 **Draw.**

 Directions: Have children observe an object with a hand lens and draw what they see.

Picture Clues

Look at the pictures.
What do you use
to measure?
What helps you
stay safe?

Let's Read
Science!

THE BIG
? What is science?

Picture Clues

(**Circle**) what the girl can use to measure.

(**Circle**) what the boy can use to stay safe.

Activity 64
Use with page 64.

 Directions: Ask children to put their finger on the picture of the girl. Have them name each object in the row and circle the object the girl can use to measure. Repeat the process with the picture of the boy, asking children to circle the object the boy can use to stay safe.

 Home Activity: Look around your home with your child. Take turns finding things you use to measure and things you use to stay safe.

Where the Wind Blows!

A cold draft blows through the room.

You shiver.

Your teeth chatter!

Where did the cold draft come from?

Find a Problem

1 Where are the windows and doors in the room?

Draw.

You cannot see the draft.

How will you find where it came from?

2 (Circle) the draft.

Plan and Draw

Wind can cause drafts.

Wind blows the wind sock.

The wind sock shows where the wind blows from.

Look at the wind sock.

3 **Draw** how the wind blows.

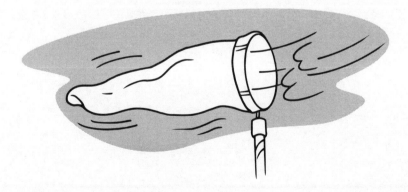

You see where wind blows with a wind sock.

4 **Draw** a tool you could make to find a draft.

14 **Plan** your tool again.

Draw how it is different.

Record and Share

12 Tell about your tool.

Did you find a draft?

 Circle

Yes	No

13 Look at a partner's tool. **Compare.**

Draw how your partner's tool is different.

11 Hold your tool near the edge of doors and windows. Does your tool move?

Draw.

Make and Test

9 **Draw** how you will use your materials.

10 Build your tool.

What questions can you ask?

You use science to learn about the world around you.

You ask many questions.

You work together to find answers.

What questions might the divers ask?

THE BIG ? What is science?

Name _____

What questions can you ask?

 Circle the picture that answers each question.

Which object is heavy?

Which animal can fly?

Which object goes around and around?

 Activity 75
Use with page 75.

 Directions: Read aloud the first question to children. Help them identify the pictures in the row. Have children choose and circle the picture that best answers the question. Ask them to explain how they figured out the answer. Repeat with the other questions.

Home Activity: Take turns with your child, asking each other questions about objects in your home and answering them. After each question and answer, talk about what you did to figure out the answer.

How do you observe?

You observe the world.

You use your senses to observe.

You use your senses to look, hear, smell, touch, and taste.

These people are using their senses.

Tell what they observe.

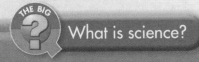

Name _____

How do you observe?

(Circle) the pictures to answer the questions.

What can you observe by looking?

What can you observe by hearing?

What can you observe by touching?

 Directions: Read aloud the first question to children. Help them identify the pictures in the row. Have children circle the object(s) that a person can observe by looking. Ask children to explain their choice(s). Repeat with the other questions. Point out that children may have to circle more than one object in a row.

 Home Activity: Choose an object in your home. Ask your child how he or she can observe the object. If necessary, ask a question about each sense—looking, hearing, touching, smelling, and tasting—and let your child answer. For example, ask: "Can you touch the object?"

How do you learn together?

You share ideas with others.

You test your ideas.

You help each other do tests.

Together you learn new things.

These children want to learn what can soak up water best.

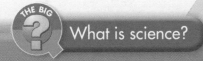

How do you learn together?

Color the picture that shows children working together.

Directions: Discuss the two pictures with children. Ask them what the children are doing and why. Then ask children which picture shows children working together. Have children color that picture.

Home Activity: Plan a task with your child, such as setting the table. First, talk about the task and decide how to divide the work. Then do the task. Afterward, talk about how planning and sharing helped with the work.

You share what you learn.
You write and draw.
You talk and show pictures.

Water

No water

Name _____

How do you share what you learn?

Think of something that moves.

Share what you know about it.

 Draw a picture of it.

 Activity 78
Use with page 78.

Directions: Ask children to think of something that moves. It could be an animal, an object, or a person. Explain that children will share what they know about this topic with others by drawing a picture of it. Encourage them to include as many details as possible in their picture. Have children take turns displaying their pictures and telling about them.

 Home Activity: Tell your child about something you learned today. Ask your child to tell you about something he or she learned in school today. Point out that you have both shared what you learned.

What do you use to observe?

You use tools to observe.

You use tools to measure.

You use tools to write and draw.

Tools help you learn.

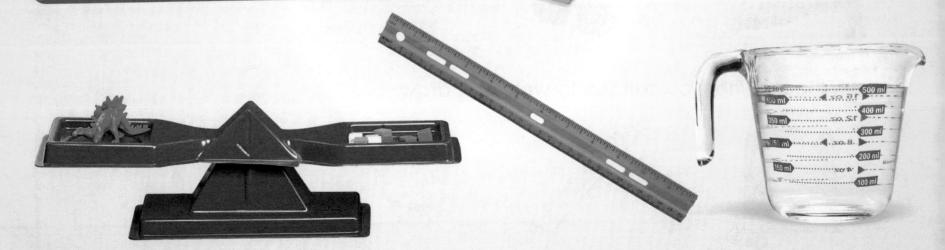

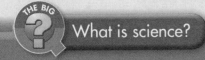

Name _____

What do you use to observe?

Circle the tool that you can use to look at things.

Circle the tool that you can use to measure.

Circle the tool that you can use to write and draw.

Activity 79
Use with page 79.

 Directions: Read aloud the first direction to children. Help them identify the pictures in the row. Have children choose and circle the object that they can use to look at things. Ask children to explain their choice. Repeat with the other directions.

 Home Activity: With your child, make lists of *Tools for Looking, Tools for Measuring,* and *Tools for Writing and Drawing.* Start with the tools on the page. Add other tools as you and your child think of them.

How do you stay safe?

Rules and tools can help keep you safe.

You follow safety rules in science.

What tools help you stay safe?

Safety Rules

1. Listen to your teacher.

2. Tie your hair back.

3. Use safety tools.

4. Handle all tools carefully.

5. Wear safety goggles.

6. Wash your hands.

THE BIG ? What is science?

Name _____

How do you stay safe?

(Circle) the picture that shows a child following a science safety rule.

Activity 80
Use with page 80.

Directions: Remind children of science safety rules. Then read aloud the direction to children. Have children circle the picture showing a child following a science safety rule. Then discuss the rules depicted.

Home Activity: Talk with your child about safety rules in the home. Together make a list of rules and post the list where everyone can see it.

How do things look?

You need

journal

viewer

plastic cup with water

objects

1 Look.

 Draw.

2 Pour.

3 Look

 Draw.

Name _____

How do things look?

 **Draw.**

How Things Look	
No Water	**Through Water**

 Directions: Have children observe an object outside the viewer and then inside the viewer. Have children compare the two views.

Student Inventor

Inventors observe their world.

Inventors make things for the first time.

Christen Wooley is an inventor.

Christen was twelve years old
when she invented a backpack vest.

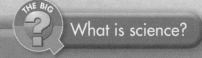

THE BIG
? What is science?

Name _____

Student Inventor

Circle things you could carry in a backpack vest.

 **Directions:** Review Christen Wooley's invention with children. Discuss how the vest can be used to carry things to and from school. Talk about the kinds of things children put in backpacks. Explain that they could put the same things in the backpack vest. Then have children circle objects they could carry in it.

 Home Activity: Play a game of "put it in the backpack" with your child. Point to an object and ask your child if you can put it into a backpack. Anything can go in the backpack if it can fit inside and is not too heavy. Your child should say no to a chair but yes to a small stuffed animal, for example.

Solve Problems

How did they make the in-line skates?

How can you solve problems?

Part 2

Name _____

How can you solve problems?

(Circle) the picture that shows in-line skates.

Draw a picture of someone skating with in-line skates.

 Directions: Discuss the opening page. Then have children circle the pair of skates that are in-line skates. Finally, have children draw a picture of someone wearing in-line skates.

 Home Activity: Your child is studying science and technology. Show your child pictures of old and new technologies, such as telephones, cameras, and music players.

What can this object do?

You need

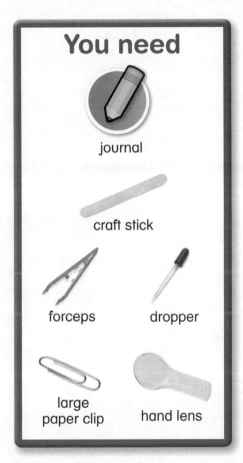

journal

craft stick

forceps

dropper

large
paper clip

hand lens

1 Look.

2 Choose.

Draw.

3 Tell.

4 Compare.

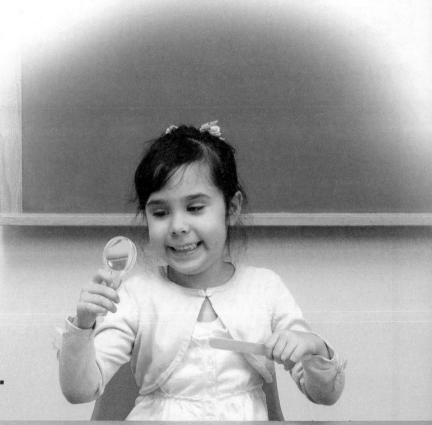

Name _____

What can this object do?

Choose.

 **Draw.**

 Directions: Have children use the hand lens to look at the forceps, dropper, craft stick, and paper clip. Then have children draw what they see.

Let's Read
Science!

Cause and Effect
What made the light turn on?

Cause and Effect

Look at what happened in each row.

Circle the picture that shows why it happened.

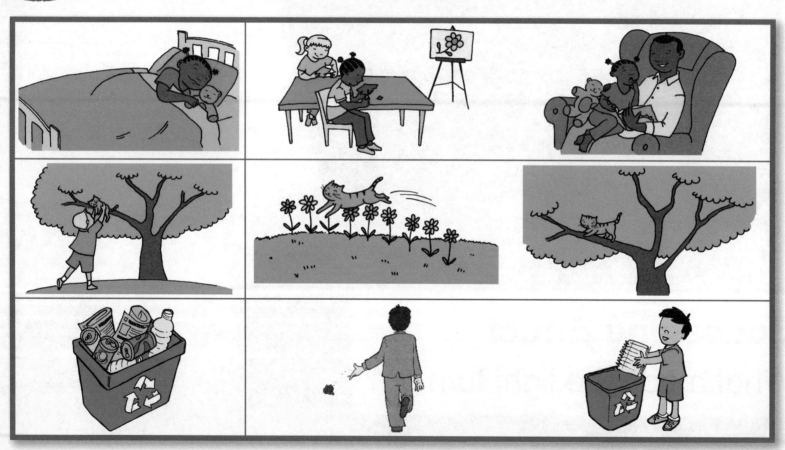

Directions: Tell children that the first picture in each row shows what has happened. Have children tell what they see in the first picture in row 1. Then have children circle the picture that shows why the girl is asleep in bed. Continue the same way for rows 2 and 3.

Home Activity: Help children point out cause-and-effect relationships in their everyday lives. For example, your teeth are clean and healthy because you brush them.

How Can You Make a Crayon Box?

Crayons roll all over the table.

Where will you put them?

Find a Problem

1 What does your desk look like?

Draw.

2 Circle the problem.

Plan and Draw

3 How many crayons do you have?

Write. _____

I have _____ crayons.

4 How big is a crayon?

Draw.

5 What will your crayon box look like?
Draw.

Choose Materials

6 Write.

Materials

7 **Draw** one material you will not use.

Tell why.

Make and Test

8 **Draw** how you will use your materials.

9 Build your crayon box.

 Do all the crayons fit in your crayon box?

Circle

 Does your crayon box hold together?

Circle

Record and Share

12 Tell about your crayon box.

Did it work?

13 Look at another crayon box.

Draw or tell how it is different.

14 **Plan** your crayon box again.

How is it different?

What problem can you solve?

You might spill when you drink from a glass.

This is a problem.

A straw is the solution.

Many straws are plastic.

THE BIG ? How can you solve problems?

Name _____

What problem can you solve?

Look at the problem in the first picture.

Circle a solution to the problem.

 Directions: Help children identify the problem shown in the first picture in the first row. Ask them to circle a possible solution to the problem. Repeat the procedure for the second row.

 Home Activity: Identify simple household problems, such as dirty dishes or dry plants. Ask your child to help you identify a way to solve the problem and then help you carry out the solution.

How can you make a plan?

You plan how to make a straw.

You write and draw.

You make the straw.

It works!

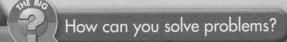

Name _____

How can you make a plan?

Think of a something you would like to make
with connecting blocks.

 Draw a plan. Show what you want to make.

Directions: Tell children that a plan shows what to make or how to make it. Then tell children to draw something they could make with connecting blocks. Encourage them to use the blocks to make what their plans show.

 Home Activity: Talk with your child about plans you use or make. You may use recipes in the kitchen or draw up a list of errands. You may follow plans for putting together a toy or piece of furniture. Show the plans to your child and tell how you use them.

How can you share your ideas with others?

You show your drawing.

You tell about the straw.

Others can use the straw too.

 How can you solve problems?

Name _____

How can you share your ideas with others?

Circle the picture of a person sharing information.

Activity 98
Use with page 98.

 Directions: Discuss with children how they can share ideas and information with others. Then have children circle the picture showing someone sharing information.

 **Home Activity:** Draw a picture of something you plan to do tomorrow, such as walk your child to school or make dinner. Share your picture with your child and discuss what it shows.

How can you lift heavy things?

You need

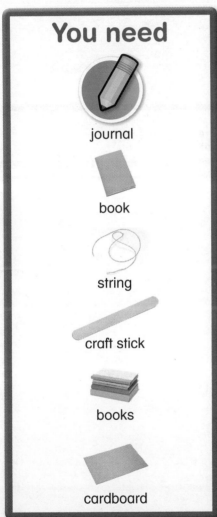

journal

book

string

craft stick

books

cardboard

1 Tie.

2 Put.

3 Pull.

4 Put.

5 Push.

6 Write.

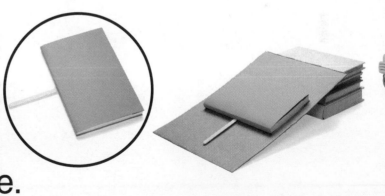

Name _____

How can you lift heavy things?

Draw.

Pull	Push

Activity 99
Use with page 99.

Directions: Have children draw how they pull the book up the ramp and how they push the book up the ramp.

Percy Julian

Percy Julian taught at a school in Greencastle, Indiana.

Percy Julian was a scientist too.

Medicine was expensive.

Percy Julian made medicine.

The medicine he made cost less.

How can you solve problems?

Name _____

Percy Julian

(Circle) the pictures that show tools Percy Julian would have used in his science lab.

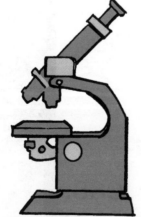

Directions: Remind children that Percy Julian was a scientist. Help them recall the tools a scientist uses. Then ask them to circle the tools Percy Julian might have used in his work as a scientist.

Home Activity: Your child learned about Percy Julian, a teacher and scientist. Ask your child to tell you about the tools scientists use in their work.

Credits

Staff Credits

The people who made up the *Interactive Science* team—representing composition services, core design digital and multimedia production services, digital product development, editorial, editorial services, manufacturing, and production—are listed below.

Geri Amani, Alisa Anderson, Jose Arrendondo, Amy Austin, David Bailis, Scott Baker, Lindsay Bellino, Jennifer Berry, Charlie Bink, Bridget Binstock, Holly Blessen, Robin Bobo, Craig Bottomley, Jim Brady, Laura Brancky, Chris Budzisz, Odette Calderon, Sitha Chhor, Mary Chingwa, Caroline Chung, Margaret Clampitt, Kier Cline, Brandon Cole, Mitch Coulter, AnnMarie Coyne, Fran Curran, Dana Damiano, Michael Di Maria, Nancy Duffner, Susan Falcon, Amanda Ferguson, David Gall, Mark Geyer, Amy Goodwin, Gerardine Griffin, Chris Haggerty, Margaret Hall, Laura Hancko, Christian Henry, Autumn Hickenlooper, Guy Huff, George Jacobson, Marian Jones, Abigail Jungreis, Kathi Kalina, Chris Kammer, Sheila Kanitsch, Alyse Kondrat, Mary Kramer, Thea Limpus, Dominique Mariano, Lori McGuire, Melinda Medina, Angelina Mendez, Claudi Mimo, John Moore, Kevin Mork, Chris Niemyjski, Phoebe Novak, Anthony Nuccio, Jeff Osier, Rachel Pancare, Dorothy Preston, Charlene Rimsa, Rebecca Roberts, Camille Salerno, Manuel Sanchez, Carol Schmitz, Amanda Seldera, Sheetal Shah, Jeannine Shelton El, Geri Shulman, Greg Sorenson, Samantha Sparkman, Mindy Spelius, Karen Stockwell, Dee Sunday, Dennis Tarwood, Jennie Teece, Lois Teesdale, Michaela Tudela, Karen Vuchichevich, Melissa Walker, Barbara Watters, Tom Wickland, James Yagelski, Tim Yetzina, Diane Zimmermann

Illustrations

ACT20, **ACT33**, **ACT36**, **ACT54**, **ACT100** Jenny B. Harris; **ACT38**, **ACT82**, **ACT83**, **ACT85** John Haslam; **ACT38**, **ACT55** Julia Wolf; **ACT64** Bob Ostrom; **ACT65** Paul Sharp; **ACT76**, **ACT98** Chris Lensch; **ACT79**, **ACT82** Michael Moran; **ACT82** Holli Conger; **ACT82**, **ACT98**, **ACT100** Ken Gamage; **ACT82**, **ACT83**, **ACT98** Leslie Harrington; **ACT82**, **ACT100** Remy Simard

Photographs

Every effort has been made to secure permission and provide appropriate credit for photographic material. The publisher deeply regrets any omission and pledges to correct errors called to its attention in subsequent editions.

Unless otherwise acknowledged, all photographs are the property of Pearson Education, Inc.

Photo locators denoted as follows: Top (T), Center (C), Bottom (B), Left (L), Right (R), Background (Bkgd)

Cover: Kirill Vorobyev/Fotolia

Front Matter

FM4 (BR) ©Ilja Masik/Shutterstock; **FM5** (CR) ©American Images Inc./Getty Images; **FM6** (CR) ©Jupiterimages/Getty Royalty Free; **FM7** (CR) ©PhotoAlto/Alamy Royalty Free; **FM8** (CR) ©Anton Vengo/Superstock, Inc.;

Chapter 1 Motion

1 ©Ty Allison/Getty Images; **3** Photolibrary Royalty Free; **6** (TL) Alexey V Smirnov/Shutterstock, (TC) Milos Luzanin/Shutterstock, (TR) Andi Berger/Shutterstock, (C) Ludmilafoto/Fotolia, (BL) Still FX/Shutterstock, (BC) Pearson Education Ltd; **14** ©Sylvester Adams/Getty Royalty Images; **15** (BL) ©Liga Alksne/Shutterstock, (BC) ©Picsfive/Shutterstock, (BCR) ©SuperStock Royalty Free, (TR) Photolibrary Royalty Free; **16** (Bkgd) Stefan Schurr/Shutterstock, (BL) Thinkstock, (BCL) Mihai Cristian Zaharia/Shutterstock, (BC) Marc Xavier/Fotolia, (BCR) ©Ilja Masik/Shutterstock; **17** (BL) Casfotoarda/Fotolia, (BR) Casfotoarda/Fotolia; **19** (Bkgd) Richard Wong/Alamy Inc.;

Chapter 2 Living Things

20 ©James H. Robinson/Oxford Scientific/Getty Images; **22** (BL) ©Chris Hepburn/Getty Royalty Free, (Bkgrd) ©image100/Jupiter, (TL) ©Kenneth Jones/Alamy Royalty Free, (BR) ©Shem Compion/Getty Images, (TCR) ©WaterFrame/Alamy Royalty Free; **33** Cultura RM/Alamy Inc; **34** ©Pierre Rosberg/Getty Images; **35** ©Tony Sweet/Getty Royalty Free, **ACT35** (L) ©Rannev/Shutterstock, (R) ©Galyna Andrushko/Shutterstock; **36** ©imagebroker/Alamy Inc.; **38** (TR) Martin Lehmann/Shutterstock, (CR) Alis Photo/Fotolia (BR) Alex533/Shutterstock; **39** ©IRA/Shutterstock; **40** (BR) JSC/NASA;

Chapter 3 Earth and Sky

41 ©Jozsef Szasz-Fabian/Shutterstock; **43** ©Joe Fox/Alamy Royalty Free; **48** (TL), Andrey Kuzmin/Shutterstock (CCL), Pearson Education Ltd, (BCL), Pamela Uyttendaele/Shutterstock (BL) Magicoven/Shutterstock, (BBL) Still FX/Shutterstock; **54** ©Galyna Andrushko/Shutterstock; **55** (Bkgd) ©Doug Chinnery/Getty Royalty Free, (TR) ©Datacraft/Getty Royalty Free, (CR) ©Galyna Andrushko/Shutterstock; **56** ©Ariel Skelley/Getty Royalty Free; **57** ©Digitaler Lumpensammier/Getty Royalty Free; **58** (Bkgd) Nbiebach/Shutterstock, (T) T. Kimmeskamp/Shutterstock, (B) DustyDingo/Alamy; **59** (Bkgrd) Randy Faris/Corbis, (T) Andy Sacks/The Image Bank/Getty Images, (B) Masterfile; **60** ©Dennis MacDonald/Alamy; **61** (Bkgd) ©Dennis MacDonald/Alamy;

Science, Engineering, and Technology Skills Handbook

Part 1 The Nature of Science

62 Photolibrary Royalty Free; **64** (T) ©Masterfile Royalty-Free; **75** ©Ian Scott/Shutterstock; **76** (BL) ©GAmut Stock Images Pvt Ltd Gamut/Alamy Royalty Free, (TR) ©PhotoAlto/Alamy Royalty Free, (BR) ©Westend61 GmbH/Alamy Royalty Free, (TL) Getty Royalty Free; **79** (TR) Image Source/Getty; **80** (Bkgrd) ©Shannon Fagan/Getty Images; **82** Christen Wooley;

Part 2 Solve Problems

85 DKCenteraTest/Dorling Kindersley Ltd; **96** (R) ©Fancy Collection/SuperStock Royalty Free; **97** (Bkgrd) ©Asia Images Group/Getty Royalty Free, (BL) Serhiy Kobyakov/123RF; **98** (R, L, C) ©Anton Vengo/SuperStock, Inc.; **100** ©Blend Images/SuperStock Royalty Free, (Inset) ©Frank Miller/Time & Life Pictures/Getty Images.